Plants

Flowers

Patricia Whitehouse

www.raintreepublishers.co.uk
Visit our website to find out more information about Raintree books.

To order:
☏ Phone +44 (0) 1865 888066
🖷 Fax +44 (0) 1865 314091
🖳 Visit www.raintreepublishers.co.uk

Raintree is an imprint of Capstone Global Library Limited, a company incorporated in England and Wales having its registered office at 7 Pilgrim Street, London, EC4V 6LB – Registered company number: 6695582

Edited by Charlotte Guillian and Harriet Milles
Designed by Joanna Hinton Malivoire
Picture research by Elizabeth Alexander
Originated by Raintree
Printed in China by South China Printing Company Ltd.

ISBN 978 1 4062 1139 9 (hardback)
13 12 11 10 09
10 9 8 7 6 5 4 3 2

ISBN 978 1 4062 1144 3 (paperback)
13 12 11 10 09
10 9 8 7 6 5 4 3 2

British Library Cataloguing in Publication Data
Whitehouse, Patricia, 1958-
  Flowers. - 2nd ed. - (Plants)
  1. Flowers - Juvenile literature
  I. Title
  575.6
A full catalogue record for this book is available from the British Library.

Acknowledgements
We would like to thank the following for permission to reproduce photographs: Alamy pp. **4** (© Phil Degginger), **12** (© M.Brodie), **16** (© PhotoStock-Israel), **18** (© inga Spence), **19** (© Keith Glover), **21** (© Frank Blackburn); Corbis p. **13** (© Frans Lanting); GAP Photos pp. **9, 23** (Dave Zubraski), **10** (Andy Small); Photolibrary pp. **8, 23** (Christopher Fairweather/Garden Picture Library), **11, 23** (Westend61/Creativ Studio Heinemann); Science Photo Library p. **17** (Geoff Kidd); Shutterstock pp. **5** (© luri), **6, 23** (© Pakhnyushcha), **7** (© Donald R. Swartz), **15** (© Kulish Viktoriia), **14** (© SNEHIT), **20, 23** (© Tatiana Grozetskaya).

Cover photograph of a dahlia reproduced with permission of GAP Photos Ltd./Marcus Harpur. Back cover photo of a sunflower reproduced with permission of GAP Photos (Dave Zubraski), and stem, Shutterstock (© SNEHIT).

We would like to thank Louise Spilsbury for her invaluable help in the preparation of this book.

Every effort has been made to contact copyright holders of material reproduced in this book. Any omissions will be rectified in subsequent printings if notice is given to the publishers.

Contents

Some words are shown in bold, **like this**. You can find them in the glossary on page 23.

What are the parts of a plant?

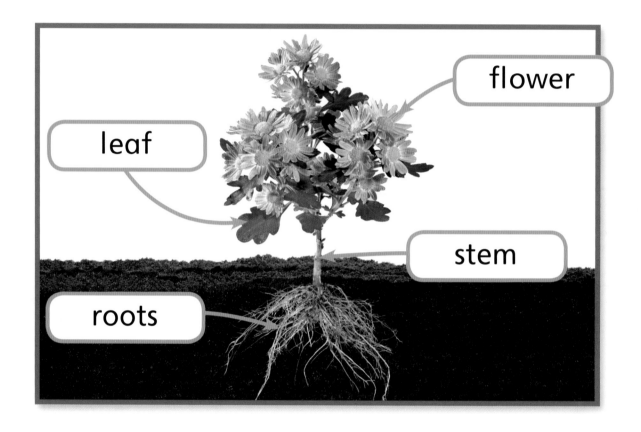

flower

leaf

stem

roots

There are many different kinds of plants.

All plants are made up of the same parts.

Some plant parts grow below the ground in the soil.

Flowers grow above the ground in the light.

What are flowers?

stem

Flowers are an important plant part.

They grow on the ends of **stems**.

Flowers grow on some trees, too.

These are the flowers on a
cherry tree.

How do flowers grow?

bud

Flowers grow inside **buds**.

Buds are flowers that have not opened yet.

petals

Buds need sunlight to open them up.

When a bud opens, you can see the colourful **petals** of the flower.

Why do plants have flowers?

seed

Flowers make **seeds**.

Seeds start to grow in the base of the flower.

seeds

petals

fruit

The flower **petals** die and drop off.

Then a fruit grows with the seeds inside it.

How big are flowers?

Flowers come in many sizes.

The forget-me-not in this picture is tiny.

Some flowers are very big.

The rafflesia is the biggest flower
in the world.

How many flowers can plants have?

Some plants have one flower.

Tulip plants grow a single flower at the top of their **stems**.

Some plants have many flowers.

The lilac plant grows hundreds of flowers at once.

What do flowers smell like?

Some flowers give off smells.

Many flowers smell nice.

These flowers smell horrible!

They are called skunk cabbage.

How do people use flowers?

People use some flowers for food.

When you eat broccoli, you are eating flowers.

People use some flowers to make perfume.

People also give flowers as gifts.

How do animals use flowers?

Some birds and insects use flowers for food.

They drink a sweet juice called **nectar** from the centre of the flower.

Some insects and spiders hide
inside flowers.

They can hide there because their
colour matches the flower.

Count and record

This bar chart compares the number of petals on different flowers.

Can you see which type of flower has the most petals?

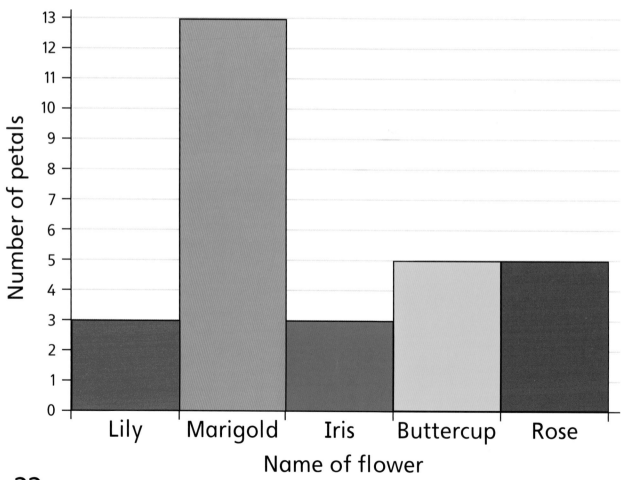

Glossary

 **bud** a flower or leaf that is still tightly closed

 **nectar** the sweet juice inside flowers that birds and insects like to drink

 **petal** the coloured or white outer part of a flower

 **seeds** the part of a flower that new plants come from

 **stem** the part of a plant where the buds, leaves, and flowers grow

Index